WINDOWS *on*
Christmas

BILL CROWDER

Discovery House.
from Our Daily Bread Ministries

Discovery House is affiliated with Our Daily Bread
Ministries, Grand Rapids, Michigan.

Requests for permission to quote from this book should
be directed to: Permissions Department,
Discovery House, P.O. Box 3566,
Grand Rapids, MI 49501.

Unless otherwise indicated, all Scripture is taken from the
New American Standard Bible © 1960, 1962, 1963, 1968,
1971, 1972, 1973, 1975, 1977, 1995 by The Lockman
Foundation, La Habra, California.

Interior Design by Sherri L. Hoffman

Library of Congress Cataloging-in-Publication Data

PRINTED IN THE UNITED STATES OF AMERICA
Fifth printing in 2016

⚛

For our children,

*Matt (and Jamie), Beth,
Stephen (and Kimberly), Andy, Mark,*

because Christmas is still about the kids.

CONTENTS

ACKNOWLEDGMENTS

❧

I never cease to be amazed at the privilege of putting words on paper. To be allowed to enter the stream of ideas that have been collected, put into print, and presented for the purpose of challenging the hearts and minds of men and women is a daunting privilege, and not one to be taken lightly.

It is also not a task to be undertaken alone. It is only because of the help and skills of wonderful people that the ideas that percolate in my heart make it to print in a way that will be, hopefully, valuable to you, the reader. That is why I hope that before you read the rest of this book, you will read the rest of these acknowledgment pages.

The creative team at Discovery House Publishers is a group that I am honored to be identified with. They are great partners in ministry, and great professionals in their craft. From Carol Holquist (publisher), Bob DeVries, and the DHP Publications Committee, who were kind enough to approve this project, to the wonderful editors, Judith Markham and Annette Selden, who help my heart find words (and are probably cringing at the length of this sentence), to Peg Willison, who proofs the copy and combs out the errors, to the support team of Kathy Comer, Judy Grothause, Melissa Wade, and Kim Fowler, these are not just colleagues—they are friends for whom I am utterly grateful to God.

It is also a task that requires a different kind of support from my family. In recent years our kids have slowly begun leaving home, but each of them has made and continues to make an impact on my heart that will never fade away. That is why this book is dedicated to them—Matt and Jamie, Beth, Steve and Kimberly, Andy, and Mark.

And above all is my life companion—my wife, Marlene—who is the true north that keeps me from losing my balance and my perspective, and who loves me in spite of my frailties and failings. Thanks, darlin'.

And in a book like this it can never be an afterthought to give thanks to the Christ who came, and who lived, and who died, and who lives forever. In Him is life, and hope, and joy—the message of Christmas wrapped in infant flesh. I can only hope that what follows here pleases Him.

Introduction

❦

$\mathcal{I}$ am a Christmas junkie. I love everything about it—the trees, the lights, the food, the gifts, the songs, the food, the celebrations, the traditions, the food, the special worship opportunities, the family gatherings, and, yes, the food. Our family, like most families that celebrate Christmas, has developed its own traditions, and each of those expressions of joy brings its own shading and flavoring to the celebration of the birth of Christ. Each one gives another layer of experience, and provides another slant and perspective on the familiar Christmas story and its celebration.

Life is all about perspective, and our own perceptions can be clarified and enriched by seeing life's events through a number of different windows. The more familiar something is, the more valuable these windows become. A fresh look, a different angle can revolutionize our appreciation of truth that might be in danger of growing stale and tired. This reality was underlined for me in a fascinating way by filmmaker

Clint Eastwood. As a lifelong history buff, I anxiously awaited his film *Flags of our Fathers*, about the World War II battle on the small Pacific island of Iwo Jima, and I was not disappointed. I learned things that I had never known about that historic fight and its even more famous flag-raising. But it was all from the perspective of the Americans fighting there. Eastwood followed this with a second film, however. *Letters from Iwo Jima* told the same story, but from the perspective of the Japanese soldiers entrenched there. Eastwood let us look through their eyes by following the letters they wrote to those at home, as they described the awful conditions and intense fighting that took place there. The two films recount the same battle, but the vision of the conflict is very different. It was an important lesson to me on the value and significance of perspective.

In the Christmas story, this fresh look can be found in the familiar Scripture of Luke 2. There we find six different perspectives on the events of the nativity, and we can share these perspectives by looking through the windows provided by those who were there, allowing us to see and feel what they saw and felt, and to learn from their responses to these wonderful and powerful events. These timeless wonders:

- Call us to kneel at a humble manger—and anticipate the horrors of a cruel cross.
- Teach us the glory of the incarnation—and the tragedy of human sin that required a Savior who would bear our sins in His own body.
- Allow us to celebrate the miracle of birth—and rejoice in the miracle of new birth.

In short, they allow us to enter into events that altered forever the world and its inhabitants—to join the humble worshipers who welcomed Christ at His birth. They give us what we often need most—fresh perspective.

THE WINDOW *of* EXALTATION

The Angels

*C*hildhood impressions are hard to shake. My dad loved huge Christmas trees, and he made quite a production of trimming those trees (a tendency that also was hard-wired into my own genetic code). First we would wrap all the lights on the tree, then cover it with ornaments and tinsel. Then I would watch as Dad placed the angel on the top branch—the final act of the tree trimming ritual. It seemed such a grand gesture. Only moments before the tree had somehow appeared incomplete, as if something important was missing. But with the placing of the angel, the house was finally ready for Christmas.

Of course, as I remember it, the angel was blonde, feminine, winged, and robed in a white gown that sparkled. For years afterward, whenever I thought of angels, my mind envisioned that figure on the top of our Christmas trees. What a shock it was, years later, when I learned that whenever angels are named in the Bible they have masculine names, and that it is highly unlikely they were blondes in sparkling gowns!

Yes, it is hard to shake our childhood impressions.

Still, I was right about one thing: angelic beings played a significant role in the events of the Nativity. Without their involvement, there would be a hole in the story—incomplete as an unfinished Christmas tree. And to help us understand the role of angels in the Christ's birth, let's take a closer look at the heavenly beings themselves.

WHO ARE ANGELS?

If you were to ask me that question in the context of everyday life, my knee-jerk response would probably be, "They are my favorite baseball team, and they play in Anaheim, California. And, by the way, they won the 2002 World Series over the San Francisco Giants." Unfortunately, much of the current cultural thinking about who angels are and what they do is no more biblically accurate than that. From paintings to poems to movies to television shows, it seems that angels need a new press agent. They just aren't being well-represented. Of course, it helps to remember that their best and most accurate representation comes to us in the pages of the Bible.

Angels are seen throughout the Scriptures and are called by a variety of names, including *cherubim, seraphim,* and *living creatures.* Sometimes they are described as men, often in shining garments. They are seen guarding Eden, waging war, rescuing Peter from prison, worshiping in the presence of God, and, tragically, in the case of some angels, rebelling against God. They carry names like Michael ("Who is like God"), Gabriel ("warrior of God"), and Lucifer ("light bearer," before he became Satan—the Adversary). They are the often mysterious, sometimes mercurial servants of God that are at the center of many of His dealings with men and women in the Bible.

The word *angel* itself comes from the Greek term *angelos*, which is defined as "a messenger, envoy, one who is sent, an angel, a messenger from God." The primary definition is *messenger*, and that is exactly what they often are seen doing in the pages of the Bible:

- Sometimes they carry a message of warning, as with Sodom and Gomorrah (Genesis 19).
- Sometimes they carry a message of rescue, as with Shadrach, Meschech, and Abednego in Nebuchadnezzar's fiery furnace (Daniel 3).
- Sometimes they carry a message of instruction, as with Hagar, Sarah's handmaiden (Genesis 16).

In each of these instances where we see angels active on earth, they are delivering messages from

God. While angels unquestionably do more than simply carry messages, it is impossible to underestimate their critical role as messengers making announcements from heaven to earth. The gospel (good news) was first delivered to the world by angelic messengers during the events surrounding the birth of the Savior.

HOW ARE ANGELS PART OF THE CHRISTMAS STORY?

So, we come back to my childhood Christmas tree. Why an angel on the top of a tree? Certainly some people use a star, but many, like my family, use an angel. Why? Because the Christmas story is filled with angels, busy carrying messages to people who are integral to the story.

The first angel we encounter in the story is Gabriel, an archangel—apparently the highest ranking in the command structure of the angelic realm. Gabriel visits planet earth to inform the principal players, and, ultimately, the world that the "fullness of time" has come—that long-awaited moment in history when the promised Messiah will arrive (Galatians 4:4). This comes in a series of announcements:

Announcement #1

The coming of the forerunner of Messiah, John the Baptist (Luke 1:5–22).

Gabriel appeared to Zacharias, an aged, childless priest who was performing his priestly functions in the temple. At first the old priest was troubled by this phenomenon, but the terror of the moment turned to comedy when he heard the angel's message. Gabriel declared to Zacharias that he and his wife Elizabeth would have a son who would be the fulfillment of Malachi's prophecy. (Malachi had promised that God would send an Elijah-like figure who would prepare the way for the messianic Redeemer.) When Zacharias, understanding the physical realities faced by himself and his aged wife, questioned the possibility of a senior-citizen childbirth, Gabriel informed him that he would be mute until the child, who was to be named John, was born.

Gabriel's announcement came true, and John the Baptist arrived to "prepare the way of the Lord"—step one in the process of bringing Christ into the world.

Announcement #2

Six months later, Gabriel came to the village of Nazareth to give a message from God to a young woman named Mary (Luke 1:26–38).

The Angels

Gabriel informed Mary that she had been selected for the role that had long been the desire of Jewish women—the privilege of giving birth to the promised Messiah. Her response was one of submissive confusion: she was ready to do the Lord's bidding but mystified as to how such a thing could occur. She was a virgin, and, being betrothed to her fiancé Joseph, had no intention of violating her vows of purity. The angel assured her that she would in no way violate her vows, and that the child would be the result of the miraculous intervention of the Holy Spirit. Furthermore, when the child was born, He was to be named "Jesus" ("the Lord is salvation")—defining both His character (as the Son of God) and His mission (as Redeemer). At that point Mary's response was one of simple availability: "Behold, the bondslave of the Lord; may it be done to me according to your word" (Luke 1:38).

Following his visit to Mary, Gabriel also visited her husband-to-be, Joseph, and gave him the same message—Mary's child was of God, not man (Matthew 1:20–25). Joseph could take her to be his wife with full confidence in her purity.

Nine months later Gabriel returned with yet another message—this time not a message of anticipation, but one of arrival.

Announcement #3

The angel of the Lord (presumably Gabriel) appears in the Judean skies over the shepherds' fields of Bethlehem (Luke 2:9–14).

The shepherds of Bethlehem were enduring yet another cold night tending the sheep when they suddenly beheld a brilliant, heavenly light show! This time the glory of the Lord accompanied the angel's message, and the shepherds were terrified by the sight. And the message itself could not have been more dramatic.

> The angel said to them, "Do not be afraid; for behold, I bring you good news of great joy which will be for all the people; for today in the city of David there has been born for you a Savior, who is Christ the Lord. This will be a sign for you: you will find a baby wrapped in cloths, and lying in a manger" (Luke 2:10–12).

These simple herdsmen clearly were not equipped to handle this! Angels were supposed to appear to priests, not shepherds. They should be calling on the current managers of the temple in Jerusalem, not men and boys who were at the lowest level of the Jewish social strata.

The Angels

We have heard this story so many times that we have become inoculated against its power and majesty. We talk about angelic appearances like they were an everyday occurrence — but they weren't then, and they aren't today.

No one could have anticipated that such an audience would be the first to hear the angels give the *euangelios* — the good news of the Savior's arrival!

WHY DO THE ANGELS RESPOND WITH EXALTATION?

Up to this point in the Christmas story the angels have served as God's messengers. But carrying messages is not the only function of angels. In fact, it may actually be secondary to their primary activities in heaven — praise and worship. Notice how this plays out in both the Old and New Testaments:

- The prophet Isaiah was transported into the throne room of God where he witnessed the angelic worship of God in heaven as the six-winged seraphim declared the glory and greatness of God:

    "Holy, Holy, Holy, is the Lord of hosts,

The whole earth is full of His glory"
(Isaiah 6:3).

The role of the seraphim is the perpetual worship of God, exalting the beauty of His holiness.

- The apostle John was given a glimpse of the
  heavenly landscape (Revelation 4–5). He saw
  the "living creatures" (another term for angels)
  declaring the holiness of God and calling on the
  redeemed to worship God for the wonder of His
  creation and to worship Christ for the grace of
  His salvation (Revelation 4:11; 5:12). All the
  residents of heaven then joined the anthem as
  they praised the Father and the Son for their
  powerful intervention into a fallen world.

Whereas in Revelation 4 and 5 the angelic realm
celebrates God's creation and Christ's salvation, in
the Christmas story they assemble in a glorious mass
choir to celebrate His invasion of the broken planet
that is the object of His eternal love (Luke 2). When
the angel announces the arrival of the Son of God in
human form, the heavenly host can remain silent no
longer. They raise their voices in exaltation of God
for His glory, for His Son, and for His plan to rescue
the lost, tired, and confused race of men and women

who, like the sheep guarded by the angels' bedouin audience, had long since gone astray. This response of exaltation becomes the great thread of worship that began that first Christmas and continues in our worship today. Their message was powerful:

> And suddenly there appeared with the angel a multitude of the heavenly host praising God, and saying,
>
>> "Glory to God in the highest,
>> And on earth peace among [those] with
>>   whom He is pleased" (Luke 2:13–14).

What Isaiah and John witnessed in the sanctuary of heaven, the shepherds experienced on that Bethlehem hillside. They heard the angels affirm the glory of God and announce that Christ had come to offer peace with God to a race in rebellion against Him. The reconciliation between God and mankind—the solution for the human condition of sin—is summed up in the simple word *peace*. It is important, however, to understand that this peace is not simply the absence of conflict—it is the presence of the Christ who is described by the prophet Isaiah as the "Prince of Peace" (Isaiah 9:6). It is, through Christ, the reality of relationship with the God of peace (Philippians 4:9). The Hebrew word for peace, *shalom*, encapsulates this idea, for it carries the weight of such realities as completeness, soundness, and contentment. Peace. The angels could offer this promise of peace to the shepherds (and us) because the Christ who makes such peace available to us had just arrived on planet earth!

The voices of the angels, raised in exaltation of the living God, continue to ring out in our celebrations today. The hope of peace, the longing for glory, the gift of Jesus. All these things that reverberated in the hearts of those shepherds continue to resonate with the deepest longings of our own hearts two millennia later.

How Did the Angels Serve the Christ?

How disappointed the shepherds must have been when the glorious bright angels left and the sky returned to its cold darkness. But the angels were not finished. They would continue to be involved in the ministry of Christ for the next thirty-plus years, particularly during critical moments of danger or declaration:

The Angels

- **An angel warned Joseph to take the Christ child out of Herod's reach:** "Now when they had gone, behold, an angel of the Lord appeared to Joseph in a dream and said, 'Get up! Take the Child and His mother and flee to Egypt, and remain there until I tell you; for Herod is going to search for the Child to destroy Him'" (Matthew 2:13).

- **Angels served Jesus following His testings in the wilderness:** "Then the devil left Him; and behold, angels came and began to minister to Him" (Matthew 4:11).

- **An angel ministered to Jesus during His suffering in the garden of Gethsemane:** "Now an angel from heaven appeared to Him, strengthening Him" (Luke 22:43).

- **An angel opened the tomb on resurrection day:** "And behold, a severe earthquake had occurred, for an angel of the Lord descended from heaven and came and rolled away the stone and sat upon it" (Matthew 28:2).

- **Angels announced the resurrection of Christ:** "The angel said to the women, 'Do not be afraid; for I know that you are looking for Jesus who has been crucified' . . . and she saw two angels in white sitting, one at the head and one at the feet, where the body of Jesus had been lying" (Matthew 28:5; John 20:12).

- **Angels attended the return of Jesus to heaven**: "And as they were gazing intently into the sky while He was going, behold, two men in white clothing stood beside them. They also said, 'Men of Galilee, why do you stand looking into the sky? This Jesus, who has been taken up from you into heaven, will come in just the same way as you have watched Him go into heaven'" (Acts 1:10–11).

Paul may have been considering a similar cataloging of the activities of angels in and around the earthly mission of Christ when, in writing to one of his young ministry protégés, he gave a summary statement of the incarnation of Christ in 1 Timothy 3:16:

By common confession, great is the mystery of godliness:

He who was revealed in the flesh,
Was vindicated in the Spirit,
Beheld *by angels*,
Proclaimed among the nations,
Believed on in the world,

The Angels

Taken up in glory.

There was great interest among the angelic host concerning the earthly mission of the Lord of glory. The events of the incarnation were not merely "seen by angels"; these divine activities were "beheld"—that is, gazed upon—with great interest. In other words, Christ's redeeming work was, and is, an ongoing source of fascination for the angelic company. Notice how the apostle Peter describes this:

> It was revealed to them that they were not serving themselves, but you, in these things which now have been announced to you through those who preached the gospel to you by the Holy Spirit sent from heaven—*things into which angels long to look* (1 Peter 1:12, emphasis added).

What does it mean, these "things into which angels long to look"? Bible teacher and commentator Adam Clarke described it this way in his commentary on 1 Peter:

> [They] stoop down to—the posture of those who are earnestly intent on finding out a thing, especially a writing difficult to be read; they bring it to the light, place it so that the rays may fall on it

as collectively as possible, and then stoop down in order to examine all the parts, that they may be able to make out the whole. There is evidently an allusion here to the attitude of the cherubim who stood at the ends of the ark of the covenant, in the inner tabernacle, with their eyes turned towards the mercy-seat or propitiatory in a bending posture, as if looking attentively, or, as we term it, poring (over) it. Even the holy angels are struck with astonishment at the plan of human redemption, and justly wonder at the incarnation of that infinite object of their adoration. If then these things be objects of deep consideration to the angels of God, how much more so should they be to us; in them angels can have no such interest as human beings have.

Why is this so? Because it involves "the incarnation of that infinite object of their adoration"—the Son of God, Jesus Christ. The angels exalt Christ for who He is and for what He has done. They exalted Him in His birth, ministered to Him in His life, supported Him in His anguish, announced Him in His resurrection—all because He is the Christ. All because He chose to do all of that for an undeserving, sin-stained race. All because He chose to express His inexpressible love

in such a mysterious and wonderful way—and pour it out on His wayward creation.

The angels know what we too easily forget: that the Lord Jesus Christ is ever and always deserving of the highest exaltation. And, as Clarke said, if the angels, who can only observe redeeming love but never experience it, exalt the Christ for His grace, how much more should adoration of the Savior drive the hearts and passions of the men and women who have been granted this great grace!

This marriage of awe and exaltation from observing angels and redeemed humanity finds wonderful expression in one of the most familiar of Christmas hymns:

> *Hark! the herald angels sing,*
> *"Glory to the newborn King:*
> *Peace on earth, and mercy mild,*
> *God and sinners reconciled!"*
> *Joyful, all ye nations, rise,*
> *Join the triumph of the skies;*
> *With th'angelic host proclaim,*
> *"Christ is born in Bethlehem!"*
> *Hark! the herald angels sing,*
> *"Glory to the newborn King!"*

May we, with grateful hearts, join in the exaltation of the Christ, God's glorious gift to us!

THE WINDOW of WONDER

Mary

One of the most haunting Christmas songs is the folksy, airy tune "I Wonder as I Wander." In the tone and style of a spiritual, it speaks of the mystery of the Christmas story and the miraculous intervention of God. It tries to express in word and note how difficult it is for the human heart to understand what God chose to do—and why He chose to do it.

> *I wonder as I wander out under the sky,*
> *How Jesus, the Savior, did come for to die.*
> *For poor ornery people like you and like I . . .*
> *I wonder as I wander out under the sky.*

I can't imagine a more appropriate word to describe that miracle than *wonder*. But I suspect that, in our world today, wonder isn't all that *wonder*-ful anymore. A recording artist who flops after his first recording is considered a "one-hit wonder." One of the plainest white breads on the market is known as Wonder Bread, and we even have Wonder undergarments. Yet somehow these things don't seem to represent an appropriate use of the word *wonder*.

The Seven Wonders of the Ancient World (such as the Great Pyramids of Giza and the

Hanging Gardens of Babylon) may more closely capture the essence of wonder—something that overwhelms the mind, reminding us that we are too small to think and process things at a certain level. But even those great and often mysterious engineering feats fall short. They were, after all, created by humans just like us. We may not know quite how they did it, but there is an explanation for it, even if that explanation is yet undiscovered.

No, *wonder* needs to be reserved for that which is beyond human explanation. *Wonder* speaks of omnipotence and omnipresence and creative power. *Wonder* speaks of God. So thought the songwriter who penned the words:

> *There's the wonder of sunset at evening,*
> *The wonder of sunrise I see.*
> *But the wonder of wonders that fills my soul*
> *Is the wonder that God loves me.*
> *Oh, the wonder of it all,*
> *The wonder of it all.*
> *Just to think that God loves me!*

Why on earth (or in heaven for that matter) would God love me? That defies understanding. I know me, and frankly I'm not all that lovable. So why would He do that? Wonder.

But to add even more to the sense of wonder surrounding that love, why would He love me the way He did—sending His Son to die for my sins and in my place? That is the very essence of the Christian faith, and there is no easy answer, aside from the nature of God Himself: love.

Because the wonder of God's love found its fullest expression in the coming of Christ on our behalf, let's look at the Christmas story through the perspective of a young woman who had more cause for wonder than any other person involved in the story.

THE WONDER OF PRIVILEGE

An American Express credit card ad used to say, "Membership has its privileges." They promoted their credit card by appealing to the human desire for being select and elite, for having an opportunity that others could only imagine. The world is divided between the haves and have nots, between the welcome and the excluded, between the privileged and the outsiders. People on the outside look in with envy and awe as the lucky few access their "privileges."

Some privileges, however, are more than just a special treat or a membership card. They carry with them the sense of amazement that you have been selected above all the rest. I don't believe I ever understood this until I met Marlene, the young woman who later became my wife.

Marlene and I had been dating less than two weeks when, while eating dinner together, she said she needed to tell me something. The somber tone of her voice made me assume that I was about to hear about the boyfriend back home or the fiancé in the military, but that wasn't the case. She wanted to tell me that she was adopted. After heaving a huge sigh of relief, I asked her to fill me in on the details. After listening to her explain how she had gone from being Kathy in Washington County, Virginia, to Lili Marlene in Raleigh, North Carolina, I asked her, "Have you ever wanted to find your real parents?"

"These *are* my real parents," she said. "They had an entire orphanage full of kids needing a home — and they chose me. They could have chosen anyone, but they chose me. *Me.*"

For Marlene, privilege was the joy of being chosen!

I suspect that young Mary felt the same way when the angel Gabriel told her that she had been chosen to give birth to the Christ child. Ever since the promise of a Messiah had been given, young Jewish women had longed to be selected for this privileged role. Centuries came and went, and no Messiah arrived. Then, the message came: the time had come for Messiah to be born, and Mary was to be His mother! Even in Gabriel's greeting, the wonder of privilege is clear: "'Greetings, favored one! The Lord is with you'" (Luke 1:28).

Luke tells us that Mary was "perplexed," and that she "pondered" at the meaning of such a strange greeting. These are strong words! *Perplexed* means "deeply distressed" and *pondered* comes from the same word as our word *dialogue.* She was, in fact, reasoning with herself, in her own mind, about the meaning of all this.

Sensing her confusion, Gabriel explained it further:

> "Do not be afraid, Mary; for you have found favor with God. And behold, you will conceive in your womb and bear a son, and you shall name Him Jesus. He will be great, and will be called the Son of the Most High; and the Lord God will give Him the throne of His father David; and He will reign over the house of Jacob forever; and His kingdom will have no end" (Luke 1:30–33).

"Found favor" meant that Mary was privileged. Talk about wonder! And Mary's response—that she was a virgin—shows how difficult it was for her to grasp such a thing. Gabriel reassured her that even as her cousin Elizabeth had become pregnant in her old age, the God of the impossible was capable of granting this privilege to her. Awe and wonder dissolved into trust and willingness of heart. Her response to Gabriel was firm and direct: "'Behold, the bondslave of the Lord; be it done to me according to your word'" (Luke 1:38).

The New Living Translation puts it this way: "I am the Lord's servant. May everything you have said about me come true."

Amazingly, Mary understood the magnitude of what she had been chosen to do, and she accepted with humility. Imagine her emotions, her disbelief, her sense of unworthiness, her joy, her amazement. Imagine the wonder in her heart.

❧

THE WONDER OF PREGNANCY

Marlene and I have five children, and their births— each of those precious children—remain the most miraculous things I have ever witnessed. It is amazing to see a baby enter the world. To hear the heartbeat for the first time and wonder whether the child is a boy or a girl. To see the ultrasound and feel the kicks of the unborn child. To watch the miracle unfolding behind the veil of the mother's body. To see that child take its first breath. Few things in life compare to that for sheer wonder.

The Scriptures are largely silent about the nine months Mary carried the incarnate Christ, but we can make some assumptions based on what we know about life. It would have been a time of new experiences in which Mary felt things she had never before known. She had no frame of reference for what she was feeling, physically and emotionally, with every day of the baby's growth. Added to that, she undoubtedly had to endure the looks and whispers of her neighbors in the village of Nazareth—ordinary people with ordinary questions about the true father of the extraordinary child she carried. The sting of pointed words and disgusted looks must have cut her deeply. And there certainly might have been times when Mary doubted her own understanding—"Did I really see an angel? Did it all really happen like I remember, or is everyone right in what they say about me and my child?"—until the wonder was affirmed.

Mary

Early in her pregnancy, Mary traveled to the Judean hill country around Jerusalem to visit her elderly cousin Elizabeth, who was pregnant with the baby who would grow up to be John the Baptizer. The Bible does not tell us why Mary went to visit Elizabeth, but it is possible that she left Nazareth to escape the harsh looks and wagging tongues. Seeking safety and support, she sought out Elizabeth. They were two women, separated by age, but connected by family. Separated by miles, but connected by history. Both the unlikeliest women to be pregnant—one too old and one a virgin.

Upon seeing Mary, Elizabeth declared: "'Blessed are you among women, and blessed is the fruit of your womb! And how has it happened to me, that the mother of my Lord should come to me?'" (Luke 1:42–43).

Mary's affirmation had come from a most unexpected source—the unborn baby that had leaped in Elizabeth's womb at the sound of Mary's voice. Mary's response, sometimes called "the Magnificat," shows the true sense of wonder she felt at the privilege of her pregnancy:

> My soul exalts the Lord,
> And my spirit has rejoiced in God my
> Savior.

For He has had regard for the humble state
of His bondslave;
For behold, from this time on all generations
will count me blessed.
For the Mighty One has done great things
for me;
And holy is His name (Luke 1:46–49).

Mary's sense of awe at this miraculous pregnancy is clear in her eloquent response of praise, worship, and thanksgiving. The wonder of this divinely orchestrated pregnancy had grasped her heart, filling her with true and uninhibited wonder.

❧

THE WONDER OF CHILDBIRTH

When Mary was nearing the end of her pregnancy, she and Joseph began the long, arduous journey from Nazareth to Bethlehem to register in the imperial census (Luke 2:1–3). Writer Walter Wangerin, Jr. imagines the struggles of the journey this way:

They were bound for Bethlehem, the city where King David had been born one thousand years before, because Joseph was descended from the house of David.

Mary

Mary rode the donkey. Joseph had fashioned a small rolled saddle to support her back. She had nearly reached the term of her pregnancy . . . She was breathless and tired, swollen in her hands, wrists, and ankles. Her long hair had lost traces of its beauty . . . Mary was determined to go with Joseph to bear her boy in the city of his father David.

Though this is just one piece of the overall wonder of the Christmas story, I find it no small thing that, in essence, the sovereign God put the entire Roman Empire in motion for the single purpose of getting Mary where she needed to be at the moment Christ would be born. Perhaps because nothing short of an imperial edict would make a woman nearing child-birth travel eighty-plus miles on the back of a donkey (Luke 2:4–5)!

Another miracle. Another wonder.

The Kindness of Strangers

Bethlehem, the home of Joseph's family and ancestors, was a village located about five miles south of Jerusalem, not far from the foothills of the Judean desert. Upon their arrival in Bethlehem, Mary and Joseph found the small community flooded with pilgrims who had come for the census. The inn was groaning under the weight of overflow capacity, and there was no place for the young couple to sleep, let alone give birth to a child. The city of David was without shelter for the young woman who was ready to deliver.

Yet someone (according to Christmas legend and most church Christmas programs, it was the inn-keeper) was willing to go above and beyond the call of duty. He or she cared enough to make accommodation for Mary and Joseph in a stable. Though primitive, this provided them shelter from the elements, from the evening chill, and privacy from the mobs of people. That simple act of kindness guaranteed that the stage was set for the most marvelous reality of all—the Lamb of God would be born in a stable.

The Birth of the Son

> While they were there, the days were completed for her to give birth. And she gave birth to her firstborn son; and she wrapped Him in cloths, and laid Him in a manger, because there was no room for them in the inn. (Luke 2:6–7)

I am always struck by the simplicity of that description. This remarkable event is so understated, so matter-of-fact, that you could almost miss it if you blinked. So much is left unsaid that you are compelled to read it again . . . and again.

A veil of silence is pulled over the young woman as she agonizes through childbirth. The shouts of joy are left unrecorded as Joseph, apparently serving as Mary's midwife, delivers the baby and hands Him to His mother.

On one level, Mary must have experienced every wonderful emotion felt by every new mother as she held her child for the first time. But on another level she had to have been overwhelmed by the realization that this child she cuddled and nursed was the Son of God, and by the thought of what this child had come to do—rescue a lost race from their sins (including herself, His own mother). This Son—promised by an angel, conceived by the Holy Spirit, affirmed by the then-unborn John, carried in the womb to Bethlehem, and surrounded in birth by farm animals—was the One whose name would be called "full of wonder" (Isaiah 9:6).

❧

Nothing in Mary's childhood or young life could have prepared her for all this. She was a normal first-century Jewish girl from an ordinary family living in an ordinary small town. Yet with wonder and obedience she embraced the extraordinary implications of God's extraordinary plan for her life. And the wonder of her nine-month emotional roller coaster brought her to one simple response: "Mary treasured all these things, pondering them in her heart" (Luke 2:19).

"Pondering." Remember, that was also her response to the message of the angel Gabriel nine months earlier (Luke 1:29). Once again she, in her own interior dialogue, in her own mind, was trying to understand all that was happening. Today, in our technology-driven culture, we would say that she was "processing."

> Processing the fulfillment of the promise.
> Processing the culmination of the pregnancy.
> Processing the journey from her home to
>   Bethlehem.
> Processing the surroundings in the stable.
> Processing the struggle of childbirth.
> Processing the visit by simple shepherds.
> Processing the wonder of God incarnate in her
>   child.

Two thousand years later, we are still processing. Still caught up in the wonder.

Mary

When Mary birthed Jesus, 'twas in a cows' stall,
With wise men and farmers and shepherds and all.
But high from God's heaven, a star's light did fall,
And the promise of ages it then did recall.

There it is—the promise of the ages. The wonder of Christmas. The wonder of it all.

THE WINDOW *of* WORSHIP

The Shepherds

*H*ow surprised Mary must have been when a band of ragtag shepherds arrived at the stable telling of angelic hosts and "a star of wonder"—all announcing the birth of her son! Though still exhausted from childbirth, Mary must have been astonished as these simple men of the fields bowed in worship before her son and then went to tell everyone they encountered about the child they had seen (Luke 2:16–18).

The shepherds were the first to kneel at the manger, which could seem surprising, given who and what they were. Yet, there they were—worshiping the newborn Savior! So let's look through the window of worship to learn about them. By doing this, we will better understand and appreciate their reactions to what they witnessed on that cold Judean night outside Bethlehem. Knowing them better will also enable us to move beyond historical records and ancient hymns to share their experience and join in their celebration.

SIMPLE MEN WITH SIMPLE LIVES

I can think of no better statement to describe the shepherds than that they were "simple men with simple lives." The very brevity of Luke's description emphasizes this simplicity: "In the same region there were some shepherds staying out in the fields, and keeping watch over their flock by night" (Luke 2:8). Yet that one verse speak volumes about who these men were and what they did.

"The same region . . . shepherds . . ."

The region surrounding Bethlehem has been associated with shepherding since the earliest days of recorded history, and it was there that David guarded the flocks of his father, Jesse. Bethlehem was a place of pasture and, therefore, appropriate for grazing flocks. It was near "the tower of Eder" (Migdal Eder) or "the tower of the flock" (Genesis 35:21; Micah 4:8), though it is uncertain what those were. Some see the titles in reference to Jerusalem in general, and the sheep gate (through which the sacrificial lambs were taken to the temple) in particular, as the strong tower of the nation of Israel. Others view it as a reference to Bethlehem, the birthplace of Israel's shepherd-king, David. Others, however, view the "tower of the flock" literally. They believe it was the actual place in the Judean hillsides from which the ancient shepherds of Israel would watch over their flocks—precisely what they were doing the night the angelic announcement was delivered. These "shepherds' hills" outside Bethlehem formed a land of sheep and shepherds that was pastoral and practical.

Even more significant, however, is that the sheep that grazed here were not ordinary sheep. Because of their proximity to the temple at Jerusalem, the fields of Bethlehem were primarily the domain of temple sheep—the animals used in the sacrifices offered in the temple. In the first century, upwards of 250,000 sheep were offered annually as sacrifices at the festival of Passover alone! Thus, these shepherds of Bethlehem were responsible for delivering healthy, unblemished sheep to be offered on the altar of sacrifice for the atonement of sin.

"Staying out in the fields and keeping watch over their flock by night."

"The night was divided into four watches," says Bible commentator John Gill. "The even, midnight, cock crowing, and morning. They kept them alternately, some kept the flock one watch, and some another, while the rest slept in the tent, or tower, that was built in the fields for that purpose." Adam Clarke adds, "The reason why they watched them in the field appears to have been either to preserve the sheep from beasts of prey, such as wolves, foxes . . . or from bandits, which were common in the land of Judea at that time."

The life of a shepherd was a life of loneliness and labor, danger and poverty. Yet, these hardships may not have been the greatest of their difficulties. Because of their profession, shepherds were considered ceremonially unclean. Their work, among other things, required their hands-on participation in the birthing of lambs (which would bring them into contact with blood) and disposing of dead lambs (which would bring them into contact with dead bodies)—both of which made them ceremonially unclean. This resulted in them being spiritual outcasts. It seems so sad that the very individuals who were responsible for raising sacrificial lambs for the temple in Jerusalem were themselves excluded from the temple because they were considered ceremonially unclean. But these shepherds faced a two-fold dilemma, for not only were they made unclean by the nature of their work, they also were required to stay constantly with their flocks. This meant that they were unable to leave their tasks for weeks at a time, preventing them from going to the temple so that they could be cleansed. It was the kind of religious "catch-22" that often bubbles up from highly legalistic systems of spiritual thought—

and these detached, castoff workers serve as tragic examples of it.

⚘

AMAZING MOMENTS OF HEAVENLY SPLENDOR

Life is filled with "moments" that brand heart and memory. Some moments are dark and foreboding, like when I got the phone call that my father had just died of a heart attack. When I think of that moment twenty-six years ago, the emotions of loss and pain flood back over me and I feel afresh the emptiness that attacked me then.

Other moments are thrilling, like the time (actually the one and only time) I broke 80 on the golf course. To this day, I can replay every one of those strokes in my mind, finishing with a brilliant birdie on the final hole for a crowd-pleasing 76 (when you only have one of those moments you have to enjoy it as long as you can).

And then there are those rare amazing moments. For me, one of those moments occurred on my wedding day. I was standing at the front of the church with the pastor and my dad, who was my best man. The music played and the bridal party entered. The

doors at the back of the church closed for a brief
moment that seemed to last forever and then the music
changed and the doors opened—and out stepped Marlene on her father's arm. As I think about it even now,
a lump comes to my throat and I get choked up. To see
the woman I loved, radiant and beautiful in her wedding dress, coming down the aisle to marry me—*me*!
It was breathtaking and spectacular and magnificent
and humbling and overwhelming. It was a moment
of splendor.

Measured against what the shepherds saw in those
moments on the hills of Judea, I know it sounds pretty
small. Yet what I felt in that moment was not alto-
gether different from what I imagine the shepherds
were feeling—breathtaking, spectacular, magnificent,
humbling, and overwhelming *splendor*.

Luke's description challenges our imaginations
and thrills our hearts.

And an angel of the Lord suddenly stood before
them, and the glory of the Lord shone around
them; and they were terribly frightened. But the
angel said to them, "Do not be afraid; for behold,
I bring you good news of great joy which will be
for all the people; for today in the city of David
there has been born for you a Savior, who is

Christ the Lord. This will be a sign for you: you will find a baby wrapped in cloths, and lying in a manger." And suddenly there appeared with the angel a multitude of the heavenly host praising God, and saying,

> "Glory to God in the highest,
> And on earth peace among men with whom
> He is pleased" (Luke 2:9–14).

How do you even begin to consider such a thing? It is far too much to process as a whole, so I prefer to break it down into moments.

The Moment of the Messenger

The angelic messenger is described as "the angel of the Lord" who was accompanied by the "glory of the Lord" which "shone" in such a way as to terrify the shepherds (Luke 2:9). Like so many involved in the Christmas story, those poor shepherds were completely unequipped for such a sight.

The glory of the Lord was referred to as the "Shekinah," the brightness of the perfection of the all-sufficient God. It has been described theologically as the sum total of the attributes of God combined together to create brilliant, perfect light. Now, the shepherds were seeing this glory of the Lord on the hillsides around Bethlehem.

In the Old Testament, the glory of the Lord was evidence of God's presence among His people. We see this phenomenon first in Exodus 24:16: "The glory of the LORD rested on Mount Sinai, and the cloud covered it six days; and on the seventh day He called to Moses from the midst of the cloud." The people of God had gathered at Sinai to either accept or reject God's rule over them as a nation. His glory displayed His power and might.

We see His glory again at the dedication of the tabernacle, the house of worship for the wandering children of Israel: "Thus Korah assembled all the congregation against them at the doorway of the tent of meeting. And the glory of the LORD appeared to all the congregation" (Numbers 16:19) And we see it at the dedication of the temple in Jerusalem where the children of Israel had established a center for their national life and worship in the marvel that was Solomon's temple: "It happened that when the priests came from the holy place, the cloud filled the house of the LORD, so that the priests could not stand to minister because of the cloud, for the glory of the LORD filled the house of the LORD" (1 Kings 8:10–11).

The people of Israel enjoyed the presence of God in their midst — until they began to stray into idolatry and immorality. They corrupted God's house with pagan idols and dishonored His name, so God responded with chilling words through Ezekiel the prophet.

After a series of events in which God displayed the spiritual adultery of His people, Ezekiel watched as, step by step, the glory of the Lord departed from the temple, and then from Jerusalem, and, ultimately, from the people of Israel. The culminating blow is seen in Ezekiel 11:23, where we read these tragic words: "The glory of the LORD went up from the midst of the city, and stood over the mountain which is east of the city" (Ezekiel 11:23).

Following Ezekiel's grim words, the few remaining references to the glory of the Lord found in the Old Testament point to the future, with no expression of God's presence among His people until that night in Bethlehem some 600 years later. There, with the angel of the Lord, the glory returned! Returned to announce the presence of God once again among His people in the person of the Christ, who John described tellingly: "And the Word became flesh, and dwelt among us, and we saw His glory, glory as of the only begotten from the Father, full of grace and truth" (John 1:14).

The Shepherds

It is "the glory of the Lord" that evokes wonder and worship—and, in the case of the shepherds, fear. For hundreds of years, the glory of the Lord had not been seen in the land of Israel. But now, in the presence of shepherds, the glory had returned!

The Moment of the Message

Ostracized from the very religious system they helped to fuel, the shepherds were required to look elsewhere for hope. That night, they found it in the angel's message, says commentator John Gill:

> To the shepherds, the first notice of Christ's birth was given; not to the princes and chief priests, and learned men at Jerusalem, but to weak, common, and illiterate men; whom God is pleased to choose and call, and reveal his secrets to as He hides them from the wise and prudent, to their confusion, and the glory of his grace. This was a precursor of what the kingdom of Christ would be, and by, and to whom, the Gospel would be preached.

Dr. Larry Richards, author and educator, reminds us that the shepherds were uniquely equipped to be the recipients of this great privilege:

The Saviour, who was now born and lying in the quiet manger, was to be the Lamb of God. And as the Lamb, He was destined to die for the sins of the world. To die for these very shepherds as their Saviour. Perhaps shepherds, who cared for young lambs, who sat through cold dark nights in the fields to guard and protect their flocks, might understand the shepherd's heart of God the Father, might glimpse what it meant for Him to give His one Lamb for all.

From a human standpoint it is amazing that the Son of God would identify Himself with shepherds, some of the lowliest members of society and culture in that day (John 10). Yet, He described Himself as a shepherd, the protector and the pursuer of His flock. Imagine these shepherds—isolated from their people, their temple, and their national hope—discovering from the mouths of angels that they were not cast out or forgotten by God, a fact that He proved by having them be the first to hear the message of hope: "Today in the city of David there has been born for you a Savior, who is Christ the Lord" (Luke 2:11).

This message of hope to the shepherds was a message of hope to all the world. For this child born in Bethlehem would become . . .

The Shepherds

- The Good Shepherd who lays down His life for the sheep (John 10:11).
- The Great Shepherd who purchased the sheep by the blood of the eternal covenant (Hebrews 13:20).
- The Shepherd and Guardian of our souls (1 Peter 2:25).
- The Chief Shepherd who comes again for His own with the reward of a crown of unfading glory (1 Peter 5:4).

HUMBLING WORSHIP IN AN UNEXPECTED PLACE

Where do you like to worship? Some prefer a majestic cathedral, others a simple chapel. But would anyone's first choice be a stable? Yet, after hearing the message of the angels, the shepherds' first response was to find the stable where Mary had given birth to the Savior.

To me, this only confirms that our God is the God of the unexpected. And few things could be more unexpected than the King of Heaven being born in a stable.

> When the angels had gone away from them into heaven, the shepherds began saying to one

another, "Let us go straight to Bethlehem then, and see this thing that has happened which the Lord has made known to us." So they came in a hurry and found their way to Mary and Joseph, and the baby as He lay in the manger (Luke 2:15–16).

I have often heard people use various forms of the expression, "You are not defined by what happens to you, but by how you respond to what happens to you." This is true, I suspect, in areas of life both good and bad, both joyful and painful, both exciting and terrifying. How we respond measures us in ways that words fail to express.

The shepherds' response was, first, to worship, and, second, to tell what they had seen!

When they had seen this, they made known the statement which had been told them about this Child. And all who heard it wondered at the things which were told them by the shepherds (Luke 2:17–18).

Shepherds were not only the first to hear, they were also the first to tell the Christmas message. With their hearts bursting with wonder at what they had experienced, they shared that wonder with others by telling the whole amazing story—the angels and the glory and the baby.

This is true worship—to kneel before the Christ so that you are then able to stand before others and proclaim His glory and salvation. To be humbled into silence in the presence of the King, so that you can then speak boldly to all who need to hear.

To think that all of this burst forth from a worship experience in a most unlikely place, on a most unlikely night, involving some most unlikely men.

CELEBRATION FROM THE HEART

The shepherds went back, glorifying and praising God for all that they had heard and seen, just as had been told them (Luke 2:20).

"These simple men," writes commentator Adam Clarke, "having satisfactory evidence of the truth of the good tidings, and feeling a Divine influence upon their own minds, returned to the care of their flocks, glorifying God for what he had shown them, and for the blessedness which they felt . . . What subjects for contemplation! What matter for praise!"

Once outcasts, they were now embraced. Once unfit for the temple, they now stood with prophets and priests to celebrate the arrival of the hope of the ages.

Shepherds celebrating at the birth of a lamb — what could be more appropriate?

Several years ago, I led a study trip through Israel, and one of our stops, of course, was Bethlehem. We had a Bible study session at a place overlooking what is known as "the shepherds' fields," and then the group had the opportunity to spend some time shopping in Bethlehem's world-famous olive wood stores. I was one of several who bought lovely nativity sets made of olive wood. The cost of the sets depended upon the fineness of the carving. Some were so rough-hewn as to be almost abstract art, while others were so realistically crafted that they looked like the figures were actually alive.

Later, as our tour bus carried us back to Jerusalem, we once again passed through the shepherds' fields. With my wooden nativity set in hand, I thought about the events of the day and the events of the first Christmas. And as we drove through the area where angels visited shepherds and proclaimed the arrival of the King, I thought of the words of one of my favorite Christmas songs:

The Shepherds

In the little village of Bethlehem,
There lay a Child one day;
And the sky was bright with a holy light
O'er the place where Jesus lay.

'Twas a humble birthplace, but O, how much
God gave to us that day,
From the manger bed what a path has led,
What a perfect, holy way.

Alleluia! O how the angels sang.
Alleluia, how it rang!
And the sky was bright with a holy light
'Twas the birthday of a King.

Driving through those hilly fields speckled with rock, rough in terrain, and still populated by scattered sheep, these familiar words held an added richness and texture. And as I looked at the hills and tried to visualize that holy night so long ago, our guide asked the driver to stop the bus. Standing on the roadside were two young boys, no more than twelve or thirteen years of age, holding a small lamb. They were Bethlehem shepherds.

Two thousand years after the birth announcement of the Son of God was delivered to poor, forgotten, ostracized shepherds, these shepherds were still working the fields and "watching over their flocks." As the boys walked down the aisle of our tour bus, almost every person placed a hand on the head of that little lamb. It was a wonderful moment. Shepherds from the shepherds' fields presenting a lamb.

Two thousand years later, we continue to celebrate the Lamb, and we join the company of shepherds who were the first to do so.

THE WINDOW of OBEDIENCE

I love music—all kinds of music. But for years I deliberately ignored country music (perhaps a little rebellion against my West Virginia roots). Then, a few years ago, my daughter convinced me to listen to some "country," and, well, I got hooked—partly because the lyrics and writing were so clever and partly because the songs often told stories.

One of the first artists Beth had me listen to was, ironically, a fellow West Virginian. I immediately embraced this singer/songwriter because he shares with me a love for the Cleveland Browns professional football team and the West Virginia Mountaineer college football team. His name is Brad Paisley, and he is as engaging as he is entertaining. Many of his songs (like "Celebrity" or "I'm Gonna Miss Her") are knee-slappingly hilarious. Others (like "I Wish You'd Stay" or "When I Get Where I'm Going") are serious and poignant.

In that latter category is a song entitled "He Didn't Have To Be," which tells the story of a boy who is the only child of a single mom. Whenever a man asks this young mom on a date, the relationship quickly evaporates when the aspiring suitor sees that she has a little boy. Time after time, the boy watches helplessly as his mother loses what he thinks is another chance at happiness, knowing all the while that it is because of him. Then, one day, a man comes to call and, with a smile, invites the boy to come along with them on their date. A bond of love and appreciation grows between the boy and the man who eventually becomes his stepfather. Now, singing as an adult, he celebrates growing up with the love and acceptance of a stepfather who made their house a home and their twosome into a trio. Now married himself, the young man stands outside the observation window of a hospital nursery looking at his own newborn baby, with his stepfather at his side. His longing and desire and prayer? That he will be able to be half the dad his stepfather "didn't have to be."

The man he had grown to love as his father could have turned around and walked away. He had a choice, and he chose to be a dad. He chose to be what he didn't have to be. He chose to love.

This song reminds me of the Christmas story because it reminds me of a central, though silent and almost invisible, character in the drama of Christ's birth: Joseph, the carpenter of Nazareth. He, too, made choices. He, too, could have turned and walked away. Instead, he undertook willingly and obediently what could arguably be the most impossible task in the universe — to be the stepfather for the Son of God.

He was obedient, at great personal cost, choosing to be what he didn't have to be. And it all began with, as was the case with Mary and the shepherds, an angelic visitor.

$$\approx$$

OBEDIENT TO ANGELIC INSTRUCTIONS

Tradition has held that Joseph was significantly older than Mary, an assumption based on the likelihood that he was dead when Jesus began His public ministry. Perhaps Joseph had waited long to marry and now anticipated the consummation of his marriage to his young bride. Their betrothal meant they were legally bound to each other, though not yet living together as husband and wife — quite unlike today's "engagements," which can be easily ended.

Imagine Joseph's heartache, then, when he heard that Mary, his pure and godly young fiancé, was pregnant! Her apparent betrayal must have rocked his world. How could she do this? And who was the man who had participated in that betrayal?

Joseph

We are not told that Joseph had any contact with Mary personally about the matter. Very likely her father ashamedly approached Joseph with the news. Now Joseph must decide what to do. It is Matthew who fills in the blanks for us, giving us a window into the quiet character of Joseph's heart:

> Now the birth of Jesus Christ was as follows: When His mother Mary had been betrothed to Joseph, before they came together she was found to be with child by the Holy Spirit. And Joseph her husband, being a righteous man, and not wanting to disgrace her, planned to send her away secretly (Matthew 1:18–19).

The heartbroken groom-to-be weighed his options. If word of Mary's pregnancy got out, he would be publicly humiliated, an object of pity and ridicule. Yet his response was not one of revenge, or even of a demand for justice. He could have demanded that his intended bride be stoned to death for the sin of adultery—sexual promiscuity occurring during the formal betrothal period. Although there were no sexual relations between bride and groom during the betrothal period, the arrangement was legally binding and could be ended only by a divorce. Instead of revenge or retribution, Joseph looked for ways to protect Mary while still obeying the law of Moses.

His options? Death by stoning, which would publicly exonerate him, or a quiet dissolution of the marriage contract that would remove her from his life. As Joseph was wrestling with this dilemma, and apparently deciding to end the betrothal quietly, he received a special message from the same messenger that had previously paid a call on Mary:

> But when he had considered this, behold, an angel of the Lord appeared to him in a dream, saying, "Joseph, son of David, do not be afraid to take Mary as your wife; for the Child who has been conceived in her is of the Holy Spirit. She will bear a Son; and you shall call His name Jesus, for He will save His people from their sins." Now all this took place to fulfill what was spoken by the Lord through the prophet: "Behold, the virgin shall be with child, and shall bear a Son, and they shall call His name Immanuel," which translated means, "God with us" (Matthew 1:20–23).

The word "considered" ("But when he had considered") is significant. It speaks of deep meditation and intense thought, and shows the degree to which

Joseph

Joseph wrestled with the dilemma. It is also a word whose meaning is synonymous with the "pondering" Mary did after her own visit from the angel Gabriel!

An angelic messenger with a heavenly message is no small thing, and the elements of the message are overwhelmingly significant:

- Joseph's position as a descendant of the great King David, hero of Israel's past, places his stepson in the line of the royal family.
- The Holy Spirit is the source of Mary's pregnancy: "Conceived by the Holy Spirit."
- The child's name, Jesus, will describe His mission: "He will save His people from their sins."
- The child's birth will be a fulfillment of prophecy in the Jewish Scriptures, explaining not just why the child was coming, but who He was—"God with us."

The message of the angel was both good news and bad news. The good news was that Mary had not been unfaithful to him after all. He could marry her without doubts about her purity or her commitment to him. The bad news? Who would ever believe it? How could he explain to friends and family the true nature of Mary's pregnancy? Surely such a story would be seen as absurd, and he would be branded a fool for believing such nonsense. Once again, Joseph stood at a crossroads of choice—a choice between self-protection and obedience.

> And Joseph awoke from his sleep and did as the angel of the Lord commanded him, and took Mary as his wife, but kept her a virgin until she gave birth to a Son; and he called His name Jesus (Matthew 1:24–25).

Obedience was Joseph's response to a deeply difficult life situation. It was not an easy or painless obedience, and it did not come without cost. It was, however, not the only time that obedience would be the hallmark of his life.

OBEDIENT TO HUMAN GOVERNMENT

For two millennia the beginning of the Christmas story has been heralded by the familiar words, "And it came to pass in those days, that there went out a decree from Caesar Augustus, that all the world should be taxed" (Luke 2:1 KJV). This passage concisely and clearly describes the reality of the world in which Joseph lived. Rome ruled with absolute authority, and either you submitted to that power or you were crushed under its weight.

The events surrounding Christ's birth, however, also serve as an impressive reminder that human government does not operate independently or in a vacuum. Proverbs 21:1 reminds us that, "The king's heart is like channels of water in the hand of the LORD; He turns it wherever He wishes." In Galatians 4:4 we are told that "when the fullness of the time came, God sent forth His Son, born of a woman, born under the Law," and part of the "fullness of time" was a divine orchestration of the events of human history to prepare the stage for the arrival of the Christ.

Now in those days a decree went out from Caesar Augustus, that a census be taken of all the inhabited earth. This was the first census taken while Quirinius was governor of Syria. And everyone was on his way to register for the census, each to his own city. Joseph also went up from Galilee, from the city of Nazareth, to Judea, to the city of David which is called Bethlehem, because he was of the house and family of David, in order to register, along with Mary, who was engaged to him, and was with child (Luke 2:1–5).

Notice the political heavyweights involved in generating this decision: Caesar Augustus, who ruled the known world at the time, and Quirnius, who governed a chunk of that world. Yet both of them were ruled by God, the king of heaven and earth. And the entire world—"all the inhabited earth"—was placed in motion so that Mary would be where she needed to be for Christ to be born where the prophets had said He would be born.

Bible scholars differ in their opinions as to whether Mary could have been excused from the difficult (and dangerous) journey to Bethlehem for the census because of her advanced pregnancy. But whatever the legal case might have been at the time, Joseph followed the edict to the letter by going to Bethlehem to be counted in the imperial census. This may seem a small thing, but I don't think so. I think it reveals the heart of this man and his complete obedience to the One who so perfectly instructed His followers (and us) on our relationship with the "powers that be." It is an indication of a heart that recognizes the function of authority and accepts it.

Joseph

As a result of Joseph's obedience, the Son of God was born in Bethlehem, the city of David, as Micah had prophesied.

OBEDIENT TO GOD'S WORD

And when eight days had passed, before his circumcision, His name was then called Jesus, the name given by the angel before He was conceived in the womb. And when the days for their purification according to the law of Moses were completed, they brought Him up to Jerusalem to present Him to the Lord (as it is written in the Law of the Lord, "Every firstborn male that opens the womb shall be called holy to the Lord"), and to offer a sacrifice according to what was said in the Law of the Lord, "A pair of turtledoves or two young pigeons" (Luke 2:21–24).

We see Joseph's next involvement in the story in an event that was without doubt his responsibility, although he is not named in the text. It was very important to a faithful Jewish man that the requirements of the law regarding the birth of a child be honored. The Mosaic law demanded sacrificial responses and ceremonial rituals, set forth in these Old Testament mandates.

- Every Jewish male child must be circumcised. This marked them as sons of Abraham (Genesis 17). First practiced at the direct command of the voice of God, circumcision became incorporated into Jewish law through Moses as a way of keeping the people of God distinct and separate from the pagan cultures that surrounded them.
- A sacrifice must be made for the purification of the new mother (Leviticus 12). This would have taken place forty days after the birth of the child, male and female. The fact that Joseph and Mary offered turtledoves or pigeons as a sacrifice shows that they were not wealthy, as those of means were required to offer a lamb.

It would have been the father's task to fulfill the requirements of the law, and although he is not named in this passage, we can safely assume that Joseph fulfilled the expectations of the law after Christ's birth, preparing the way for the One who would later say: "Do not think that I came to abolish the Law or the Prophets; I did not come to abolish but to fulfill" (Matthew 5:17).

Joseph

The Christ who would bring all the law to its true and complete fulfillment followed in the footsteps of an earthly stepfather who took obedience to God seriously. In all he did, Joseph exemplified the spirit of submission that God expects and deserves from His children.

OBEDIENT TO A HEAVENLY WARNING

Before Joseph's final appearance in the pages of the Bible, where we find him visiting the temple at Jerusalem with Mary and twelve-year-old Jesus (Luke 2), we see him faced with two more opportunities to obey or disobey (Matthew 2).

> Now after Jesus was born in Bethlehem of Judea in the days of Herod the king, magi from the east arrived in Jerusalem, saying, "Where is He who has been born King of the Jews? For we saw His star in the east and have come to worship Him." When Herod the king heard this, he was troubled . . . (Matthew 2:1–3).

The magi's visit alarmed Herod, who viewed the birth of a new king as a clear and present danger to the stability and longevity of his own kingdom. The repercussions of the magi's visit to Bethlehem must have been equally troubling for Joseph, albeit in an entirely different way. After these mysterious strangers showed up on the doorstep, another angelic messenger alerted Joseph to the danger hanging over their head.

> Now when they [the magi] had gone, behold, an angel of the Lord appeared to Joseph in a dream and said, "Get up! Take the Child and His mother, and flee to Egypt, and remain there until I tell you; for Herod is going to search for the Child to destroy Him." So Joseph got up and took the Child and His mother while it was still night, and left for Egypt. He remained there until the death of Herod. This was to fulfill what had been spoken by the Lord through the prophet: "Out of Egypt I called My Son" (Matthew 2:13–18).

Mary and Joseph lived far beneath the notice of rulers and magistrates. The thought that their child might be in danger from such powers would never have occurred to them. Suddenly Joseph realized that they lived in a world that was far more dangerous than they ever imagined. Only an angelic voice could have convinced them that their baby boy was in danger.

Joseph

When Joseph received the warning from the angel, he didn't hesitate. His first instinct was to protect the child. The journey to Egypt would be long, and even dangerous in itself, but with Herod's threats hanging over them, they could not stay in Bethlehem. In Egypt they would be safe. And out of Egypt, Christ—like the Moses-led children of Israel hundreds of years before—would eventually return home to live and grow and prepare for His years of public ministry.

> But when Herod died, behold, an angel of the Lord appeared in a dream to Joseph in Egypt, and said, "Get up, take the Child and His mother, and go into the land of Israel; for those who sought the Child's life are dead." So Joseph got up, and took the Child and His mother, and came into the land of Israel (Matthew 2:19–21).

On a human level, Joseph's willingness to obey the angel's warning provided the first of many escapes from peril that Jesus experienced. The One who was often heard to say, "My hour has not yet come" would survive this and other threats until the moment arrived for His death on the cross—a death that would fulfill the law, remove the need of further sacrifices, and redeem a sin-filled world.

Joseph's obedience was part of the preparation for the ministry and accomplishment of the Son who "learned obedience from the things which He suffered" (Hebrews 5:8).

�֎

When we look at the story through Joseph's window we clearly see his constant heart of obedience. Facing choice after choice after choice, he responded obediently to each challenge set before him.

The beauty of obedience has been somewhat tarnished in our "have it your way" world where "doing your own thing" has become the rallying cry. Yet, there is still a simple, quiet beauty to the obedient heart. It speaks against the rebellious nature of our fallenness and points us to a better way. It shows us the wisdom of taking God seriously and the folly of self-determination. It reminds us that God is sovereign and we are not— and that this is the way it is supposed to be.

In his excellent book, *A Long Obedience in the Same Direction*, Eugene Peterson says this:

> Friedrich Nietzsche . . . wrote, "The essential thing 'in heaven and earth' is . . . that there should be long obedience in the same direction; there thereby results, and has always resulted in the

long run, something which has made life worth living." It is this "long obedience in the same direction" which the mood of the world does so much to discourage.

The "long run." A "long obedience." Joseph chose to live such a life of obedient trust in a world that discourages long-term commitment in favor of instant gratification. And, as we face the challenge to ignore or obey, to follow the Master or go our own path, Joseph leaves us an example well worth following.

We never hear Joseph speak. He doesn't initiate, he responds. He doesn't take center stage; he works behind the scenes. But the abiding characteristic of his consistent example is his willingness to obey God — because, apparently, he had long before learned to trust God. In fact, Joseph's obedience teaches us that trust and obedience are inseparable. If we do not first trust God, we will never surrender our choices and destinies to His purposes, and if we do not obey God, we will never see the great and humbling things He wishes to accomplish in and through our lives. No wonder one of the Christian faith's most beloved hymns echoes this simple truth:

> *Trust and obey, for there's no other way*
> *To be happy in Jesus, but to trust and obey.*

THE WINDOW *of* CONTENTMENT

Simeon

Years ago, I heard Dallas Seminary professor Howard Hendricks say that Christmas in America is not so much about giving as it is about swapping. If we give someone a fabulous gift, and the gift we receive from them is, well, less than fabulous, that's okay. We'll make sure that things get evened out the next year when it comes time to select their gift. Who hasn't sometimes felt just a little slighted at the inadequacy of a gift received? (Come on, be honest now.) In fact, our culture feeds that disappointment by pointing our attention to gifts that are impossible for the average person to afford. Still, we wake up on Christmas morning certain that someone, whose love for us will be measured by the quality of his or her gift to us, is going to hit it out of the park this year. How can anything but the weeds of discontent grow in that kind of emotional playing field?

For me, this drags my memory back to when I was twelve years old, the year I asked for a guitar for Christmas. My request seemed perfectly reasonable. After all, how could I become the next Paul McCartney or George Harrison if I didn't start playing? I lay awake all Christmas Eve imagining the feel of the strings on my fingers and the effortless chords that would flow from that instrument (never mind the fact that I didn't know how to play). Finally, Christmas morning arrived. I waited anxiously until Dad gave the signal for us kids to descend on the Christmas tree like a plague of locusts. Then I dashed down the stairs to the living room and looked all over for my guitar—but it wasn't there! And to make matters worse, I found in its place the worst Christmas gift any twelve-year-old boy/aspiring Beatle ever received—a dictionary!

Now, from the perspective of my alleged adult-hood, it is clear that I was never going to be the 1960's equivalent of "American Idol," and I acknowledge that I have spent my adult life dealing with words. Therefore, the dictionary was a gift that had much more enduring value and worth. But you could never have convinced a heartbroken twelve-year-old of that fact. A day intended to be a joyful day of celebration had been darkened by the cloud of disappointment. Under that cloud, speeches regarding the need to be grateful, happy, or content only exacerbated my dis-appointment. That is what comes from expectations that are either unrealistic or deceived. They will never produce contentment.

So this chapter is a rather challenging one for me because it reminds me of how selfish inappro-priate expectations can be, and how necessary it is — especially during the season devoted to God's gift to us — to recalibrate my own expectations. The challenge to cultivate a heart of contentment is a tough thing to grapple with, and millions of bad examples of wrong expectations and deep disappointment could be cited as warnings. Perhaps a better plan would be to see a single example of right expectations and the profound contentment they can generate.

❦

A LIFE OF DEVOTION

As I think of the heading for this section, the names and faces of people who have lived long lives of spiritual service and faithfulness fill my memory — people whose examples have influenced my own heart and thinking about ministry. It seems that at every critical step along the way in my own spiritual journey, I have been privileged to encounter an older saint who was walking the walk and doing the work with joy and satisfaction. While I may feel underqualified to write out of my own life about a life of devotion, I am pretty sure that I know a life of devotion when I see it. It has a lot to do with "staying by the stuff" and "buckling in for the long haul" and "running all the way to the finish line" — and all those other clichés that are made trivial because they tend to be timed with a stopwatch when what they really require is a calendar. A life of devotion demands more. It demands everything.

This next perspective on the Christmas story involves just such a man. Now in his advancing years, Simeon has been a fixture at the temple in Jerusalem for longer than anyone can remember. But he keeps showing up, honoring his God, waiting for the Promise. His devotion is captured by Luke with only a few words, but each one is packed with insight:

> And there was a man in Jerusalem whose name was Simeon; and this man was righteous and devout, looking for the consolation of Israel; and the Holy Spirit was upon him (Luke 2:25).

This man, Simeon, had a track record instead of a reputation. Notice how he is described:

- **Righteous**: In the broad sense, *righteous* refers to a person who is upright, virtuous, keeping the commands of God. It speaks of someone who is committed to living life on God's terms instead of his or her own. In a narrower sense, *Strong's Concordance* describes a righteous person as one who deals appropriately and fairly with others.

In either case, it is certainly a noble title that is worthy of our aspirations.

- *Devout*: This word speaks of a person who reveres God and allows that reverence to impact his life and his choices. Whereas *righteous* has to do with obeying God, one who is *devout* is consumed with honoring God. A significant commitment indeed.

- *Looking for the consolation of Israel*: "The consolation of Israel" is a reference to the Messiah of Israel. Simeon was living his life based on this anticipation—"looking for" the Messiah. While many, especially senior citizens, appear to be consumed with the past, Simeon was fixated on the future.

- *The Holy Spirit was upon him*: This is fascinating because until the Holy Spirit came to indwell believers at Pentecost (see Acts 2), the Holy Spirit's role was largely in the background. The attachment of the Spirit of God to an individual in this way is a New Testament phenomenon being experienced by a man living prior to the cross.

If someone could use only a few phrases to describe you, what would they be? My wife and I joke about the episode of the old TV show *WKRP in Cincinnati* where the radio station's sales manager, the terminally cheesy and slimy Herb Tarlek, is being profiled on a local television program. He has pounded into everyone how he wants to be represented, and it comically becomes a relentless mantra of untrue characterizations that he himself has scripted for all his colleagues and family members to repeat over and over—hardworking, family man, all-around good guy. That was how he wanted to be perceived; it just wasn't how he wanted to live. I prefer Luke's list. The description he gave of Simeon did not have to be fabricated. It was not a caricature. It was an accurate description of a faithful man who lived a life of devotion.

THE THRILL OF HOPE

The concept of hope is one that is, frankly, fraught with peril. It is often fluffy and without substance, having more to do with optimistic wishes than with confident expectation. That is because hope must be attached to something—or, in this case, Someone. Notice how Luke continues to weave Simeon into the Christmas picture he is creating:

And it had been revealed to him by the Holy Spirit that he would not see death before he had seen the Lord's Christ (Luke 2:26).

The simple truth is that the something to which biblical hope is attached is, in fact, Jesus Christ. This allows the reality of hope to be more than merely a "hope-so" sentimentality. This hope is rugged and strong, with the ability to empower us as we move through life. In Christ, hope becomes a significant platform from which we can launch out into the deep end of the pool, trusting Him.

Simeon's hope came from a remarkable promise that the Holy Spirit had given him:

Simeon would not see death
UNTIL
Simeon saw the Lord's Christ.

"The Lord's Christ" was "the anointed one of the Lord," the Messiah, the long-awaited hope of the ages. For hundreds and hundreds of years the Jewish people had comforted one another with the promise of Messiah and found strength in that promise during difficult days. They had cried out for its fulfillment during times of national crisis and had rested quietly in its assurance during days of national prosperity.

Now, after centuries of waiting, a signal was given: Simeon's life would serve as a line of demarcation in history. If he died, Messiah was alive somewhere on planet earth. But the second part of the promise was even more mind-blowing. Simeon would not just live until Messiah arrived; He would personally see the Promised One!

This promise radically affected the way Simeon viewed life and the way he lived his life. The impression we get from Luke's record is that, as a result of this promise, Simeon spent his days in the temple awaiting this promise and living in anticipation of the moment that he would see the Messiah of Israel. It was the same anticipation that marked the heart and spiritual passion of hymn writer and poet Fanny Crosby. Blinded in childhood, Crosby wrote with eyes that saw more spiritually than most of us ever see physically. Like Simeon, she lived a life of anticipation as she longed in hope for the time when she would see the King of Kings, which prompted her to write words that Simeon would have fully appreciated:

> *Some day the silver cord will break,*
> *And I no more as now shall sing;*
> *But, oh, the joy when I shall wake*
> *Within the palace of the King!*

And I shall see Him face to face,
And tell the story — Saved by grace.

What Fanny Crosby anticipated in heaven, Simeon was promised on earth—the hope of seeing the Lord's Christ and the world's Savior "face to face." That is something to be hopeful about!

❦

THE SATISFIED HEART

For some months Taco Bell ran a series of ads promoting their new super-gigantic burritos and tacos by having fairly ordinary people dramatically announcing, "I'm full!" The point of the ad campaign was that "ordinary" fast food couldn't fill you up. The only way to really satisfy your hunger was with one of their burritos. Of course, one candy maker would argue that to be truly satisfied you don't need a ten-pound burrito—you only need one Snickers bar, because, after all, "Snickers really satisfies." Then again, many folks would say that their experience is much more like Mick Jagger's raspy cry, "I can't get no satisfaction!" Even King Solomon, with all of his wealth and wisdom, pleasure and prestige, declared that all of life was "vanity"—emptiness. His conclusion? "So I hated life" (Ecclesiastes 2:17).

In a world where satisfaction is hard to find and harder to keep, we are driven to the Christ who said, "I have come that you might really, really live" (my paraphrase). Jesus offers a life of fullness and abundance—and Simeon was among the very first to experience it.

Notice again the reference to the ministry of the Holy Spirit in the life of this faithful man. The Spirit was with him (2:25), had revealed the promise to him (2:26), and now it was the Holy Spirit that was moving Simeon to the temple so that the promise could be fulfilled.

And he [Simeon] came in the Spirit into the temple; and when the parents brought in the child Jesus, to carry out for Him the custom of the Law, then he took Him into his arms, and blessed God, and said,

"Now Lord, You are releasing Your
    bond-servant to depart in peace,
According to Your word;
For my eyes have seen Your salvation,

Which You have prepared in the presence of
all peoples,
A light of revelation to the Gentiles,
And the glory of Your people Israel" (Luke
2:27–32).

At the outset, this must have been terrifying for
Mary and Joseph. No sooner had they entered the temple for the rituals that the law required for the birth of
a son, then out of the shadows stepped a man who took
their child from them and began making a proclamation. As bizarre as that might have seemed, what really
got their attention was the content of that proclamation.
Simeon declared the truths that they had quietly held in
their own hearts since the angelic messenger had visited
them so many months before. He also underlined the
message the angel had delivered to the shepherds in the
Bethlehem fields. Their reaction would have, reason-
ably, been one of shock and surprise.

Simeon's response, however, was one of absolute
satisfaction and contentment. The promise that had
driven him for so much of his life had been fulfilled.
Messiah had arrived. How could he ever want for
anything more? He had actually held the Christ in
his arms! He had looked into the face of God.

For years, anticipating this moment, Simeon must
have wondered about the promised encounter. Had he

imagined that he would meet the Messiah as a newborn infant? Or had he expected a royal entourage that he would glimpse from a distance? Whatever he had imagined, it could not begin to measure up to what he was blessed to experience. He had seen the Christ—and as a result experienced a fullness of life and satisfaction of heart so profound that he declared, in essence, "No more! I don't need any more! I have seen the Christ. Now, O God, let me depart from this life in peace!"

Mary and Joseph had already witnessed amazing things—angels, shepherds, the star over Bethlehem. Now, added to that was the prophetic praise of a total stranger, who proclaimed that his life was complete because he had seen their son. They could only stand there in amazement "at the things which were being said about Him" (Luke 2:33).

What a fantastic scene it must have been that day in the temple as Mary and Joseph watched a completely contented man do the most meaningful thing he would ever do—celebrate Jesus.

THE SOBER ANNOUNCEMENT

When your doctor tells you, "I have good news and I have bad news, which do you want first?" you get a sudden thud in the pit of your stomach. The first time I heard those words, the good news was that the bloodwork for my medical checkup had come back with an encouraging report: overall my health was fine. The bad news, however, was a message my body had already been sending me — a message I had chosen to ignore. Due to a hectic travel schedule abroad over several months, where I had found myself eating unusual things at weird times while under stress and pressure, my weight had climbed to a point that was, well, not good. The bad news led to further bad news that would include a rather severe (in my opinion) diet in order to correct the problem. Good news and bad news often travel together, and much of the time the messages carried by both are far more serious than a personal "battle of the bulge."

In Simeon's encounter with Mary and Joseph, he had celebrated the Christ Child and the fulfillment of the promise of God that He represented. Wonderful, miraculous, extraordinary good news. But this good news, by implication, also carried bad news for this young mother who had embarked on an adventure like no other.

What bad news could there be involving the birth of the world's Savior? Luke gives us the grim answer:

Simeon

And Simeon blessed them, and said to Mary His mother, "Behold, this Child is appointed for the fall and rise of many in Israel, and for a sign to be opposed — and a sword will pierce even your own soul — to the end that thoughts from many hearts may be revealed" (Luke 2:34–35).

That grave prophecy reminds us that the Christmas story — the joyous, glorious birth of the Savior — was only a part of the process by which He would save the world. The first steps of the journey brought the most profound joy and happiness, but the final steps would be fulfilled as Mary stood at the foot of the cross watching with tear-stained eyes and broken heart as her son — the holy one of Israel — paid for the sins of the world. Simeon's "bad news" for Mary was indeed a bitter pill, for the suffering of her Son would cut like a sword to the very depths of her soul. The pain of labor by which she received Him at His birth would be mirrored by the pain she would experience in releasing Him to His sacrificial death.

Mary must have spent the next thirty-plus years pondering that prophetic statement as Jesus grew, and, then, as He carried out His public ministry. Perhaps she watched in fear as her son entered the crowds or debated the religious leaders. Her life would be marked with anticipation, just as Simeon's had been. But while he had found contentment in the arrival of the Christ, she would feel pain and loss as that same Christ — her son — suffered and died. Simeon's lifelong anticipation resulted in joy. Hers ended in grief.

☙

Simeon's window of contentment offers us a helpful perspective, especially as we think about the way Christmas is celebrated in our western culture. The promise had been fulfilled. Simeon had seen *and held* the Savior. Yet at the heart of his response was a depth of satisfaction that can only come by experiencing the personal presence of the Christ.

What of our Christmas? Does our celebration foster gratitude and contentment, or disappointment? Is it marked by the drive to possess, or the quiet peace of knowing that "I am His and He is mine"? The spirit of the age pulls us inexorably toward consumption — especially at Christmas. But the heart of Simeon reminds us that there is more than just *more*. There is Christ, and His promise: ". . . being content with what you have; for He Himself has said, "I will never desert you, nor will I ever forsake you" (Hebrews 13:5).

Simeon

May our celebration of the Christ be defined by the unique contentment of the heart that comes from knowing Him.

THE WINDOW *of* WITNESS

At age twenty I was working for the natural gas company in our area of West Virginia. My job was in the department of civil engineering, where I worked with crews surveying pipelines, well sites, and plot maps. In January that year, we were dispatched to Fort Gay, West Virginia, to run a survey that would site a core-hole sample location where they wanted to drill for coal, in preparation for an attempted coal-gasification experiment. That winter day the weather reports said that the winds were gusting up to eighty miles an hour, which, added to the already brisk temperatures, made for an extremely frigid morning. Since I was low man in seniority on the team, I was the one who got to leave the warmth of our company vehicle and climb to the top of a railroad bridge to locate the U. S. government benchmark from which we had to begin our survey.

To this day, I am unclear about what happened next. I have always assumed that one of those eighty-mile-per-hour gusts blew down the hollow and knocked me off balance, because the next thing I remember is waking up at the bottom of the ravine in a dry creek bed below the deck of the bridge. I tried to get up and passed out again.

Anna

The next time I came to, I was in the back of our utility vehicle, headed to a hospital in Huntington, West Virginia, where the emergency room personnel spent the day taking X-rays and trying to figure out why I wasn't dead. I had fallen thirty-eight feet into a dry creek bed and landed on my neck, yet I had escaped with only a neck sprain and a slightly compressed spine.

I was in traction for a week, and in a hard collar on disability for three months. By the time I returned to work, the bosses must have determined that I was a danger to myself and everyone else, because they moved me from the field crew to the safe confines of the map room.

The most vivid memory I have of my hospital stay, however, is not the X-rays or traction, although I gained a bountiful harvest of sermon illustrations from those experiences! What I remember most was one special afternoon. Sharing my hospital room was an elderly gentleman who was already in the other bed when I was admitted. Once I was in traction, I could see nothing but the ceiling, a less than wonderful view to have for a week. But several times a day I would hear people (usually hospital staff) come to the door and whisper in hushed voices.

"Is that him?"

"Yes."

"He's the one who is supposed to be dead?"

"Yes."

"Why didn't the fall kill him?"

"No one knows."

This scene played itself out over and over. Then, one afternoon during visiting hours, as I lay there looking up at the ceiling, I heard the muffled tones of the man in the next bed talking with his wife. It sounded as if they were crying, and I assumed they had gotten some bad news from the doctor. But I couldn't have been more wrong. At the end of visiting hours, the woman came over to my bed and leaned over my face so that she could look me in the eye. She still had tears in her eyes as she said, "My husband told me what happened to you. We are Christians. We believe God spared your life because He wants to use you. We are going to pray for you to that end." Then she walked away.

I was released soon after that, and I never saw the woman again. But I have never forgotten her or the words she spoke to me that day. To that point in my life, I had done a pretty good job of living for myself. I had grown up in a church where the gospel was not presented, and the thought of God being taken seriously, let alone being interested in me, was a shock to my system. It caused me to start thinking about things I had never considered before. I started attending a church that taught the Bible, and eighteen months later accepted Christ as my Savior and Lord. And it all began with that brief, heartfelt, sincere witness from an elderly woman who didn't know me from Adam's house cat. She could have just ignored me, but she compassionately and courageously gave witness to her faith in God and her concern for me. And God used her words of witness to change my life.

When I think of that dear lady (who I look forward to seeing again in heaven), I think of Anna in Luke 2. She, too, was an older woman, spiritually committed and passionate about giving witness to Christ. I am so grateful for Anna's presence in the Christmas story, because God used an Anna of a different generation to impact my own life so powerfully.

THE WOMAN OF WITNESS

To discover Anna's perspective on the birth of the Son of God, we must begin by asking, "Who was she?" William Barclay refers to Anna as "one of the Quiet in the Land" because the Scriptures give us little information about her. Yet in just three verses we are given a fascinating snapshot of this woman. Notice how Luke pictures her and her entrance onto the scene:

And there was a prophetess, Anna the daughter of Phanuel, of the tribe of Asher. She was advanced in years, and had lived with her husband seven years after her marriage, and then as a widow to the age of eighty-four. She never left the temple, serving night and day with fastings and prayers. At that very moment she came up and began giving thanks to God, and continued to speak of Him to all those who were looking for the redemption of Jerusalem (Luke 2:36–38).

Only three verses, but they are filled with helpful insights into the woman that Herbert Lockyer labeled, "The Woman Who Became the First Christian Missionary."

Her Name and Family

The name *Anna* is the New Testament equivalent of the Old Testament "Hannah," a word that means "grace" or "favor," and Anna certainly was favored by seeing the infant Christ and telling of His arrival on planet earth.

Anna's father was Phanuel. His name means "the appearance or face of God," and was derived from the patriarch Jacob's wrestling with God. After that experience, Jacob renamed the location Penial, because he said, "I have seen God face to face, and have survived"

(Genesis 32:22–32). *Phanuel* (from *Penial*) speaks powerfully of the intimate face-to-face communion with God that is the privilege of the child of God. The intimacy, the immanence, the nearness, yes, even the accessibility of God—all of those extraordinary ideas reside in that wonderful name by which Anna's father was known—Phanuel, the "face of God."

Anna is also described as being from the tribe of Asher. Asher was the eighth son born to Jacob (Israel), and the second by Leah's handmaid, Zilpah. When he was born, Leah named him *Asher*, which means "happy." Bible historians see this as significant because Asher has often been considered one of the so-called "lost tribes of Israel." Apparently, they were not so lost after all, for in the first century Anna is clearly identified as a member of that tribe.

Her Life Situation

When I was in seminary, it was fashionable to speak about the principle of *sitz im leben,* which is German for "life setting" or "life situation." To put it simply, in the thinking of some German theologians, all of scriptural study was reduced to this one point: Does it matter in the situations of life? While that is far too general and simplistic an application of the concept, the fact remains that we live life in the midst of specific situations, and those situations mold and shape us personally, as well as molding and shaping our responses to the situations we face in life. We do not live alone on a desert island. We live life in a series of situations that impact who we are becoming in Christ. This was true of Anna, as well.

Her life situation was etched in sorrow and marked by perseverance. Widowed after only seven years of marriage, Anna was apparently left childless—facing a life without joy and a life without significance in her culture. The sorrows of her youth carried on into her old age, for she is described as being eighty-four years old and having never remarried (note that some Bible scholars translate the verse as saying that she lived an additional eighty-four years after her husband's death, which would make her about 105 years old).

The sorrow of such loss and the perseverance of long life would be a destructive combination for many people, plunging them into a perpetual black hole of despair and self-pity. But such was not the case with Anna. She chose to live positively in the service of her God—praying, praising, and anticipating His grace.

Her Consistent Priorities

What we are committed to speaks loudly about who we are and what we value. For Anna it was simple: Her priority—her goal—was pleasing God.

Anna

Although no prophets had been heard from since the days of Malachi, Anna is called a prophetess. Luke doesn't describe the nature of her prophetic ministry or the content of her prophetic message, but he offers unquestioned affirmation that she was a spokeswoman for God to her generation. After over four hundred years of prophetic silence, God chose a widow with a heart for Him to reopen His declarative expression to the world.

In conjunction with an apparently public prophetic ministry, however, Anna also participated in private worship that testified to a life devoted to God. "She never left the temple, serving night and day with fastings and prayers," writes Luke (2:37). What does that mean? In *Be Compassionate,* Warren Wiersbe says that she was so committed to waiting for the coming of the Lord that she had moved from her homeland with the tribe of Asher to Jerusalem and remained at the temple. Others say it merely means that she was a regular presence at the temple, always attending the services there. Either way, she was a fixture at the house of God and committed to spiritual discipline. Anna's life was a model of personal devotion, continually worshiping her God and continually praying and fasting.

This dear woman, whose love for God was the driving force in her life, is painted in brief, but powerful words by William Barclay:

> *She had known sorrow, but she had not grown bitter.*
> *She was old, but she had never ceased to hope.*
> *She never ceased to worship.*
> *She never ceased to pray.*

In a life situation that could easily have driven her *from* God, Anna allowed her heart to be drawn *to* God. And her years of faithfulness were rewarded, for she was in her customary place (the temple) and maintaining her consistent priorities (worship, prayer, and fasting) when the little family from Nazareth entered the temple to fulfill the demands of the law required by the birth of Jesus.

THE OCCASION OF WITNESS

At critical moments in history when the right person is matched with the right event, remarkable things happen. Such a person was Anna. Prepared by decades of spiritual devotion, she was in the right place at precisely the right time.

Anna

At that very moment she came up and began giving thanks to God, and continued to speak of Him
to all those who were looking for the redemption
of Jerusalem (Luke 2:38).

"That very moment" is the critical phrase here.
In one sense, what Anna was doing was merely the
continuation of what she had done for almost sixty
years—she was going to the temple to worship. Yet,
that is what makes it so remarkable. She had been
doing it for some sixty years! Imagine what would
have happened had she decided, "I'm tired. I've been
doing this for years. I think I'll take the day off and
stay home." But she didn't! And her faithfulness to
God positioned her in the temple at the very moment
that Simeon took the Christ from Mary's arms and
lifted Him up, declaring Him to be Israel's long-
awaited, long-hoped-for Messiah.

"This was no mere coincidence," writes Herbert
Lockyer in *All the Women of the Bible*:

Through her long pilgrimage, day after day,
[Anna] went to the Temple to pray for the coming of the Messiah, and though He seemed to
tarry she waited for Him, believing that He would
come. Then one day the miracle happened, for as

she entered the Temple she heard sounds of exultation and joy proceeding from the inner court, and then from the lips of the venerable Simeon she heard the words, "Now, Lord, lettest Thou Thy servant depart in peace, for mine eyes have seen Thy salvation." Gazing upon the Holy Child who was none other than her long-looked-for Messiah, Anna, too, was ready to depart in peace and be joined with her husband above.

I love that! Anna's years of faithfulness had been rewarded in a moment of celebration. In the right place at the right time, she saw the Christ. But she didn't stop with worshiping and giving thanks. She bore witness to what she had seen.

THE MESSAGE OF WITNESS

All of her life Anna had been a faithful worshiper and a prophetess, but now her role shifted and she became a missionary. She "began giving thanks to God, and continued to speak of Him [Jesus] to all who were looking for the redemption of Jerusalem (Luke 2:38). As Herbert Lockyer says, "Anna was one of the godly remnant in Israel who, through centuries, even in the darkest days before Christ came, looked for the Day-spring from on high. Thus, as she heard Simeon's praise for prophecy fulfilled, she went out to her godly intimates to declare the glad tidings."

Good news is not to be secreted away; it is to be shared. Anna shared the good news boldly, and her good news was "Redemption has come."

The New Testament uses several different words that are translated "redemption," explains James Montgomery Boice in *The Christ of Christmas,* and all have to do with the freeing of a slave:

- *Agorazo*: referring to the *agora,* or the market-place, where oftentimes slaves were bought and sold. Once purchased, the slave was . . .
- *Exagorazo*: bought out of (ex) the marketplace (agora) never to be sold there again. Instead that slave was to be:
- *Luo*: literally, cut loose and given his freedom.

In Anna's message of "glad tidings," Jerusalem is portrayed as the center of the world. But "the redemption of Israel" also represents the reality of the human condition. The Bible describes every human being as being enslaved to sin and without hope in the world. The Christ being proclaimed by Anna, however, had come to set free that lost human race. He came to bring redemption — *lutrosis* (from *luo,* to loose) — deliverance and rescue from sin and its penalty. Just as Hosea, the Old Testament prophet, out of the depths of redeeming love, went to the slave market to purchase his disgraced wife, Gomer, and make her his own once more, Jesus Christ came to the slave market of this broken world and purchased His bride, with a redemption sufficient for the sins of the entire world.

Anna's message was one of hope, joy, and freedom. After decades of anticipating the coming of the Redeemer King, she now found herself living in a world where this Christ had finally come. The promise had been fulfilled, so she gave thanks and went out to tell anyone who would listen that freedom and forgiveness and redemption were now available, for Christ had come. It is the message that missionaries have been taking to the uttermost parts of the earth ever since.

⁂

Looking through Anna's window, we see a reminder from the prophetess of the truth and meaning behind all of the chaos and confusion that we amiably call Christmas.

"Christmas is not merely the story of the birth of a helpless baby in a stable," writes James Montgomery

Boice, "as beautiful as that may be, not the wonder of the shepherds, not the gifts of the wise men, not the enraptured singing of the angel chorus. The heart of Christmas lies in the fact that, 'God so loved the world that he gave his one and only Son, that whoever believes in him shall not perish but have eternal life'" (John 3:16).

In the midst of all "the stuff" that surrounds our celebration of Christmas, it is far too easy to forget that the first Christmas happened because our sin demanded payment—and only Christ Himself could make a payment sufficient to cancel our debt.

While it may be fun to celebrate the holiday with gifts and ornaments and candles and parties, "the holy day" of Christmas is really about rescue and redemption. Anna knew that, and she told her world.

May we be willing to make part of our celebration of the birth of Christ a commitment to tell our world as well, for the world needs to know that:

> *Living, He loved me;*
> *Dying, He saved me;*
> *Buried, He carried my sins far away;*
> *Rising, He justified freely, forever;*
> *One day He's coming—O glorious day!*

OUR WINDOW on
Christmas

The men and women and angels that witnessed the events surrounding the birth of Christ leave to us a legacy of response, and their responses were anything but casual. They were intense and passionate as they gazed on the Christ child and glorified His heavenly Father.

The great challenge left to us, I suspect, is that all of our Christmas celebrations should include traces or threads of all the reactions they exhibited—exaltation, wonder, worship, obedience, contentment, and witness. If we do this, we will cut through all the glitz and the glam that can camouflage the Christmas Child, drowning out the noise of a season grown increasingly secular and commercial, and reminding us of the beauty of the One who *is* Christmas. These windows on Christmas are perspectives to be treasured.

We revel in the benefits and blessings of Christmas—but He *is* Christmas. We enjoy the gifts and trappings of Christmas present—but He is the eternal One who brings true joy and everlasting life. We can be consumed with wrappings and focused on lists of presents—but the One wrapped in cloths at His birth remains "the greatest Gift of all." May we look and love and never forget that . . .

Our Window on Christmas

This, this is Christ the King,
Whom shepherds guard and angels sing;
Haste, haste, to bring Him laud,
The Babe, the Son of Mary.

This Christmas day, and every day . . .

O come, let us adore Him,
Christ the Lord.

NOTE TO THE READER

The publisher invites you to share your response to the message of this book by writing Discovery House, P.O. Box 3566, Grand Rapids, MI 49501, USA. For information about other Discovery House books, music, or DVDs, contact us at the same address or call 1–800–653–8333. Find us online at dhp.org or send e-mail to books@dhp.org.

BOOKS BY BILL CROWDER

Overcoming Life's Challenges
The Path of His Passion
Singing the Songs of the Brokenhearted
The Spotlight of Faith
Windows on Christmas
Windows on Easter